the little book of
KISSES

the little book of
KISSES

Raymond Glynne

ARCTURUS

PICTURE ACKNOWLEDGEMENTS

Ardea: 9, 13, 19, 37, 49, 52, 53, 78.

Corbis: 22, 26, 34, 54, 55, 87, 90, 93, 94, 95.

Creative Image Library: 32.

FLPA: 27, 33, 35, 39, 72, 82, 85, 91.

Nature Picture Library: 18, 21, 48, 58, 64, 65, 69, 75, 89, 92.

photos.com: 23, 46.

Photoshot: 70, 83.

Press Association: 14, 42, 45, 61, 73.

Robert Harding: 11, 15, 40, 43, 62, 68.

Science Photo Library: 24, 79.

Shutterstock: 6, 8, 10, 16, 17, 20, 25, 28, 29, 30, 31, 36, 41, 44, 47, 50, 51, 59, 60, 63, 66, 67, 71, 74, 76, 77, 81, 84, 96.

Superstock: 7, 12, 38, 56, 57, 80, 86, 88.

ARCTURUS

This edition published in 2011 by Arcturus Publishing Limited
26/27 Bickels Yard, 151–153 Bermondsey Street,
London SE1 3HA

Copyright © 2010 Arcturus Publishing Limited

ISBN: 978-1-84837-762-2
AD001714EN

Printed in China

Your first kiss was probably the one your mother gave you within moments of your birth. And ever since then, you will have kissed and been kissed countless times, and for many different reasons.

A kiss can say a multitude of things. It can be affectionate, playful, apologetic, loving, tender, cursory, heartfelt. But whichever it is, the power of the kiss should never be underestimated.

So trust in this most natural of gestures and give someone a kiss today.

THAT'S WHAT LIPS ARE FOR

Lips are for loving encounters…

For tender moments...

For getting up close and personal…

For having fun…

And for the deepest affection…

Kissing can be a tricky skill to master…

And small margins can make a big difference...

It's a delicate balance between enthusiasm...

And coyness…

That holds the key to success…

The first kiss is always a nervous moment…

Should you play it cool...

Or throw yourself into it…

Don't be too eager to please…

But remember that practice makes perfect…

Great kissers make it look easy…

A good kiss requires perfect balance…

For that feeling of bliss…

Contentment…

And just a hint of indulgence…

Kissing doesn't always come naturally…

Some make it look harder than it really is...

Sometimes it's too sloppy…

Or just too complicated…

But persistence brings its rewards…

It's good to have something in common…

Whether it's hairstyles…

The way you dress…

A laid-back attitude to life…

Or simple animal magnetism…

A beak needn't be a hindrance…

And kissing shouldn't ruffle any feathers…

In fact, it can sometimes be pure joy...

Just start with a little peck…

But beware of overdoing it…

Looks aren't everything…

Everyone's got an admirer somewhere...

You'll always find love amongst family…

Just make sure you're approachable…

And take your opportunities when they come...

A lingering kiss is a moving experience…

Love can be all-consuming…

An intense binding force…

A spur of the moment thing...

Which can take you to another place...

Friends come in all shapes and sizes…

And a kiss can make you feel ten feet tall…

So aim high…

And move in the right social circles…

Because everybody needs friends in high places…

Try to kiss with grace…

Poise…

Artistry…

Flexibility…

And, above all, affection…

Of course, there are unwelcome advances…

You can grin and bear it...

Gaze into the distance…

Close your eyes and wait for it to pass…

Or speak out in protest…

Tenderness is a kiss on the cheek…

Or a nibble on the nose…

A spontaneous show of affection…

That stops you in your tracks…

And is strangely addictive…

A kiss is the key that unlocks dreams…

It's a tender moment in a hectic day…

When you close your eyes, all your troubles fade away…

You can let yourself unwind…

As long as you don't get too relaxed...

On the other hand, eyes can say so much…

They can draw you in deeper and deeper…

A hypnotic cord between the two of you...

Though eye contact can become a bit too intense…

You might even have to look away…

Some kisses are obtained by stealth…

In the most unexpected places…

Out on a limb…

Seizing the moment…

For a fleeting fond farewell…

It can be tricky to find the One...

And the more you try…

The more you put your foot in it...

They say that opposites attract…

And sometimes it's the most unlikely partnerships that work...

When you kiss, the world doesn't matter any more…

It's just the two of you...

Forgetting all the social conventions…

Taking strength from one another…

In a world of your own…